Mothering

Em Coley

Curate, St Mary's Parish Church, Wendover

GROVE BOOKS LIMITED
RIDLEY HALL RD CAMBRIDGE CB3 9HU

Contents

Acknowledgments

I would like to thank Barry Hill, fellow student at Wycliffe Hall who first suggested that I should consider publishing my Mothering Sunday essay and to Carolyn Headley my liturgy tutor for her encouragement. Many thanks also to Trevor Lloyd, Tim Stratford and particularly Christopher Byworth from Grove for all their help putting this booklet together.

The Cover Illustration is by Peter Ashton

First Impression October 2005
ISSN 0144-1728
ISBN 1 85174 603 X

Preface

1

This year at St Mary's Church in Wendover we didn't give out posies on Mothering Sunday!

For a while now I have been convinced that the way we as a church celebrate Mothering Sunday, and especially the practice of handing out posies to women (often regardless of whether they are mothers) makes the day particularly difficult and often inappropriate for many people. This year, instead, St Mary's considered 'mothering' in a broader non-gendered way that enabled us to focus on all those who mother or care for us.

After the sermon, in which I had preached about comfort (a God of comfort, the comfort we receive from others and the role we have in bringing comfort to others) we had a basket of chocolates at the front of church. The congregation was invited to come up, take a chocolate and give it to someone to say thank you for the care and comfort they had given. The children came up first, most of them to take a chocolate for their mums, followed by the adults. Many of the adults told me who they were taking the chocolate for: 'This one is for Joan—she does a lot of mothering in this church'; 'these are for my two daughters for all they do to look after me.'

People, regardless of their own personal circumstances, had been affirmed, encouraged and thanked

From my vantage point at the front of church I witnessed lovely encounters between various people—people giving and receiving thanks. Perhaps the most moving exchange happened right at the end when a father of two made his way to the front of church where Mark (the vicar) was standing, to give him a gift to thank him for the mothering Mark does for all of us. At the end of the service there was a fantastic atmosphere of love, support and unity as people, regardless of their own personal circumstances, had been affirmed, encouraged and thanked. It was a great way to celebrate Mothering Sunday.

I remain convinced, therefore that we need to put a lot of thought into how we as a church can celebrate Mothering Sunday in a way that makes it accessible and appropriate for as many people as possible.

2

How can we make Mothering Sunday an appropriate celebration in the church today?

Mothering Sunday is a key date in the church's calendar. It is a day which celebrates the role of mothers, a role that is so often taken for granted in our society. It is a day which brings families into church, many of which would not otherwise attend Sunday services. Yet it is a day which causes much pain for a lot of people. Would it not therefore be easier if the church were to avoid raising the profile of mothers on this one day of the year?

Would it be easier if the church were to avoid raising the profile of mothers on this one day of the year?

As we consider this question, it is important to acknowledge the difficulties facing mothers today. A survey commissioned in 1996 by the Joseph Rowntree Foundation opens with the statement:

Family life in 1990s Britain is characterized by change and uncertainty. The increased employment rates of mothers, continuing high levels of male unemployment, and the insecurity associated with the 'flexible' labour market all have implications for the ways mothers and fathers provide for their children's material needs and allocate time to their family roles.[1]

The survey goes on to suggest that fathers are generally working longer hours, that although dual-earner families are in the majority there is a distinct lack of day-care provision, and that even when both parents are in full-time employment mothers take on major responsibility for domestic life. Family life is increasingly being put under pressure.

In this time of social change, where women are becoming more likely to have children and a job, when gender roles are less defined, being a mother is an increasingly difficult role to take on. It is also a role that is often overlooked and taken for granted. It is important therefore for

It is important therefore for the church to set aside a special day in order to honour mother

the church to set aside a special day in order to honour mothers. Similarly, with single parent families and divorce rates on the increase and the prevalence of dysfunctional families, it is also important for the church to celebrate a day that affirms families and brings them together.

However, as has already been suggested, the issue is not this simple for, as chapter 7 discusses, Mothering Sunday is also a particularly painful day for many other groups of people. The question, 'how can we make Mothering Sunday appropriate today?' is a highly pertinent one. In answering this question it is important to consider the three traditional elements in Mothering Sunday: Mother Church, Mary Mother of God and our mothers, as well as the notion of God as our Mother, whilst asking how the church can honour mothers without inflicting unnecessary pain. The history of Mothering Sunday, in particular its name and origin, sheds light on the original focus of the day, and to this we now turn.

3 The History of Mothering Sunday

The Origin of Mothering Sunday

There is much confusion surrounding the origin of Mothering Sunday, possibly because there are a number of unconnected strands within its historical development. It is important to understand the chronology of the historical development, as it reveals that the tradition with which we are most familiar today was the last to be introduced.

1 A Heathen Custom

The reason for the celebration of Mothering Sunday during Lent originates from our pagan ancestors. The Ancient Greeks and the Romans both held a festival in the spring to honour motherhood. The Romans celebrated the feast of Matronalia in order to honour the goddess of motherhood, whilst the Greeks held a festival on the Ides of March in honour of Cybele the mother of the gods.[2] When the church was established in Britain, however, the focus was changed to honour Mother Church.[3] Some customs involved in these festivals were retained, namely sons and daughters giving their mothers cakes and flowers, but Mother Church took the place of the goddesses.

2 Mother Churches

Probably some time after the Norman Conquest, the practice of daughter churches visiting the Mother Church of the diocese was introduced.[4] This custom, which was highlighted in Brady's *Clavis Calendria* published 1815, was a well-established practice, yet as Constance Penswick Smith (a pioneer of the 19th century who strived to prevent Mothering Sunday becoming a purely secular custom) comments 'the exact date of the introduction of this custom is enveloped in the mists of antiquity.'[5] Part of the reason for the visit by the members of the daughter church to the Mother Church was to take an offering for presentation at the altar. Smith links these visits to the tribes of Israel making pilgrimages to the Holy City and argues that we must now consider the 'Minster' to be the Mother Church, the family home. She draws on the ideas of a Revd E Cutts who suggests that the reunions would promote the idea of brotherly communion and Christian unity, in the same way that the attendance of the Israelites on the three great festivals of their one Temple in Jerusalem tended to maintain the national unity of the people as the people of God.[6]

It is interesting that although visiting the Mother Church on a set Sunday in Lent played a significant role in the establishment of Mothering Sunday, it is a tradition that has been lost and most people today are not aware that it used to be customary. As Cutts has indicated, however, it is a tradition that the intermingling of congregations would focus the church on the issue of unity. This will be discussed in more detail in chapter 4.

3 Visiting Home

The common understanding of Mothering Sunday is that it grew out of a secular custom established in the 18th and 19th centuries when domestic servants were given the day off to visit their homes and mothers. This is a misreading of the custom, for it does not indicate that the visit to parents was a by-product of the dutiful visit to the Mother Church. It was these annual visits to the Mother Church that brought families together. Thus Smith asserts, 'the family festival in honour of earthly mothers grew up with the religious observance of the day.'[7] It seems important to acknowledge that whilst our society has secularized Mothering Sunday, emphasizing sending cards and flowers and visiting home, originally the day was a religious observance, a church-orientated custom.

The Mothering Sunday Movement

Reclaiming Mothering Sunday for the church was the reason for the 'Movement for Mothering Sunday' started in 1913. The Movement was based on the assumption that once people understood the significance of Mothering Sunday they would want to go a'mothering (the old-fashioned term for visiting mothers and presenting her with a gift) and would frustrate all attempts to secularize the custom. In many ways the Movement was successful, for Mothering Sunday is still an important day on the church's calendar and the tradition of visiting mothers or sending gifts still remains. There is still, however, an element of the fight against secularization to be had. This is evident even in the wording of the day's title, referred to by general society as Mother's Day, whilst appearing in the church calendar as Mothering Sunday.

This restriction of mothering to mothers impoverishes the meaning of the day and is less than true to its origins

This restriction of mothering to mothers impoverishes the meaning of the day and is less than true to its origins.

But the controversy surrounding the day is broader than this church versus secularist debate, for the concern is now also how the church can observe and celebrate Mothering Sunday without alienating those for whom it is a painful day.

4

Mother Church

The church chooses the occasion of Mothering Sunday to think about and give thanks for the church as mother, Mary Mother of God and our mothers.

The focus on Mother Church is not now understood to be a reflection of the custom of visiting Mother Churches, but relates to the BCP Epistle of the day, Galatians 4:21–31, in particular verse 26: 'The other woman corresponds to the Jerusalem above, she is free, and *she is our mother*.' Biblical commentators today differ about whether this is an allusion to the church. J D G Dunn for example suggests, 'It would be a mistake to make anything like a straight identification of "the heavenly Jerusalem" with the church.'[8] Historically, however, stalwarts of Protestant doctrine have argued for a clear parallel; thus Luther, writing on the back of centuries of Christian tradition, stated, 'the heavenly Jerusalem is the church which is now in the world.' A traditional understanding of Galatians 4:26 thus explains why the church has been called Mother Church.

Historical Approaches to 'Mother Church'

The church fathers were keen on the concept of Mother Church and between them Tertullian, Cyprian, Origen and Augustine all affirmed, albeit with different renderings, the notion that 'You cannot have God for your father unless you have the church for your mother.' As Carl Braaten, a modern biblical scholar explains:

> For the ancient fathers the notion of church as mother was more than a beautiful phrase and lovely metaphor. It signifies identity as we are offspring of the bride of Christ; it signifies nourishment as from her hands we receive food and drink, the very body and blood of our Lord Jesus Christ.[9]

This theme of the church's nourishment is evident in Calvin's *Institutes of the Christian Religion* as he too advocates the importance of understanding the church's role in sustaining her 'children':

> We may learn even from the title mother, how useful and even necessary it is for us to know her; since there is no other way of entrance into life, unless we are conceived by her, born of her, nourished at her breast, and continually preserved under her care and government till we are divested of this mortal flesh, and 'become like the angels.'[10]

Calvin goes on to emphasize, however, that it is not the church that achieves salvation or remission of sins. He is keen to disassociate the church from a salvific role, whilst still acknowledging that she plays an important part in the life of the believer. One of Calvin's disciples, Philip du Plessis-Mornay, affirms that this maternal understanding of the church relates directly to our understanding of God as father. He suggests that it is God's will that the church is honoured and recognized as Mother by all those who call him 'Father.'[11]

As modern Protestantism has developed, this view has changed as can be seen in Frederich Schliermacher's description of the antithesis between Protestantism and Catholicism. He argues that whilst Protestantism makes an individual's relationship to the church dependant to his or her relationship to Christ, Catholicism makes an individual's relationship to Christ dependant on his or her relationship to the church.[12] It is a generalization, but perhaps a fair one, to suggest that Protestants are significantly less affirming of the notion of Mother Church. Interestingly, however, it is Catholics who are more aware of the dangers or the negative connotations of viewing the church as mother.

A Nagging and Restrictive Mother?

Sally Cunnee, an American Catholic, author of *Mother Church: What the Experience of Women is Teaching Her* writes largely affirmingly of the church as Mother. Yet she is keen to point out the negative impact this understanding has had. Just as many people have experienced difficult and damaging relationships with their mothers, so many have had negative encounters with the church. Many Catholics will say that the church they experienced was not asking them to grow or giving them greater freedom, but limiting them and preventing their faith maturing. Cunnee's view is that when she uses the image of Mother Church many people react negatively:

> They think of a nagging mother who accentuated the negative — 'Keep away from sin' — and passed on her fears of what was outside her own fortress of authority. Such a mother was apt to be so intent on inculcating doctrinal truths and mandating goodness that she made a real relationship with her grown-up children impossible.[13]

Because of these negative experiences, both of the church and of human mothers, Mother Church is a concept that many simply do not accept as credible, whilst for others it emphasizes negative maternal characteristics.

Church Unity and Mothering

Whilst acknowledging the negative connotations of viewing the church as Mother, there are positive implications. These appear to be twofold, that of church unity and that of mothering in general. Carl Braaten's book, whilst considering the development of the understanding of Mother Church, focuses mainly on the issue of ecumenism and church unity. He writes of *Mother Church: Ecology and Ecumenism*:

> Its chapters tell the story of my own growing awareness of the place of the church in the divine scheme of things. I write in the conviction that Protestants...need to rediscover the idea and experience of the church as mother which characterized the fathers of the ancient church.[14]

Braaten is writing in 1998, yet even as early as 1932, Constance Penswick Smith had recognized the impact on church unity of accepting the church as our mother. She considered that if Christians are all members of one family, then the church is logically the mother. She longed to see the observance of Mothering Sunday create in congregations a great desire for unity, and a rejection of dispute and disagreement.[15] With the growing secularization of our society, the church's need for unity is sharper than ever before; incorporating this element into Mothering Sunday must be a positive step forward.

Mothering Sunday would be an appropriate day on which all churches in a benefice could join together for a united service

It seems that Mothering Sunday would be an appropriate day on which all churches in a benefice could join together for a united service. It would be possible with the joint congregations not just to affirm those who mother us, but the united church of the benefice, the diocese and even the church worldwide. There could be a helpful emphasis during the prayers on churches abroad with which the benefice has a particular link, or simply praying for the mission and witness of the church throughout the world.

Another positive aspect to come out of the notion of Mother Church is the wider concept of mothering itself. Cunnee recognizes the need to re-examine the term 'Mother Church.' She argues that the metaphor needs reinterpretation because of what contemporary psychology, recent history and theology have taught us about 'mother' and 'church,' and our sounder understanding of gender differences and of mothering.[16] Cunnee claims that whether male, female, parent or non-parent we all 'mother' other people throughout our lives.

She defines mothering as:

> a human virtue, a self-confidence that facilitates an enlargement of sympathy and leads to thinking and action in the interest of others.[17]

In our society today, 'mothering' is an often unmet need, both on the part of those who need to feel loved and nurtured, and by those who long to lavish love and care onto others. Is it not logical that the church should play a part in providing opportunities for mothering? As the people of God we *are* Mother Church in as much as we must endeavour to nurture one another, to keep trying to empower and enable growth, and to avoid being over protective and stifling. This teaching is surely highly appropriate for Mothering Sunday and in its inclusivity enables men and non-biological mothers to consider the important issue of mothering.

As the people of God we are Mother Church in as much as we must endeavour to nurture one another

With this in mind, Mothering Sunday is a suitable day in which to exhibit the care we have for one another within both the congregation and the wider community. There could be a special emphasis for the congregation after the service, or during a extended time of intercession, for people to pray for one another, sharing their current situations, concerns and joys. It would also be a fitting day for prayer-triplets or prayer chains to be promoted. A demonstration of Mother Church's care for the wider community could be undertaken as the congregation visits or takes meals to the lonely or isolated in the community, or indeed puts on a lunch to which these people are invited. The church could do a 'rubbish mission' around the community, clearing places of rubbish or debris—a practice which would certainly be appreciated by the community as a whole. If we are to take seriously the role we have to care for, or 'mother,' others then we need to give time to the practical outworking of this calling.

5

Mary, Mother of God

> What a tragedy it is that the mother of the one whom all Christians honour as the Saviour of the world should herself be such a problematic figure among the churches.[18]

So laments David Wright in his introduction to *Chosen by God: Mary in Evangelical Perspective*. He goes on to suggest that part of this controversy is due to the impression gained from Roman Catholics that Mary is at least as important as Jesus. Sadly, this reaction against the Catholic idolization of Mary may have resulted in the rejection of what we still can learn from her:

> As Christians observe Mother's Day, their thoughts appropriately turn to an archetypal mother: to the mother within whose flesh Divinity became flesh. Ever since the Reformation, Protestants have tended, in their scorn for Madonna-worship, to ignore what all Christians can learn from her. Mary's experiences were unparalleled in human history; yet at significant points they can provide a pattern for all Christians.[19]

Is it possible then, on Mothering Sunday, to move beyond this rejection of Mary in order to make some helpful sense of Mary, Mother of God?

'Mary, Mother of God'

The title, 'Mother of God' was not commonly used until the late 5th or early 6th centuries, a fact which David Wright deems to be slightly strange, especially considering Elizabeth's question in Luke 1:43, 'And why has this happened to me, that the mother of my Lord comes to me?' Throughout history, the reactions to the title 'Mother of God' have been diverse; the Reformers were divided in their opinions and Calvin in particular objected to it. However, 20th-century theologian Karl Barth writes in favour of such a description: 'The description of Mary as "Mother of God" was and is sensible, permissible and necessary as an auxiliary Christological proposition.' Barth's argument is based on the affirmation of Christ as truly human as well as truly divine, and thus the importance of affirming his human mother. The controversy surrounding this term has not been resolved, yet today the question seems to branch further out, as we consider the appropriateness of remembering the person of Mary on Mothering Sunday.

Theological and Sociological Responses

At this point it is important to acknowledge the Catholic position on Mary. The Second Vatican Council outlined two of Mary's fundamental roles as co-redemptrix and intercessor. The Vatican Council concurred with Ireneaus' assertion that Mary 'became the cause of salvation for herself and for the whole of the human race.'[20] The council goes on to suggest that as death came through Eve, life came through Mary. The Protestant faith, however, is concerned to limit the implications of Mary's role. Whilst recognizing Mary as mother of Jesus, the suggestion that the salvation that comes through Jesus also comes through Mary is to negate the uniqueness of Christ and his saving act, and in Wright's terms threatens to expand the Trinity into a quaternity.[21]

Mary is also credited with the role of intercessor. The Vatican Council encourages all people to persevere in their prayers to Mary, in the belief that through her intercession the nation will come to the knowledge of truth.[22] This again is not a practice undertaken by the Protestant church.

In contrast, the Protestant church emphasizes two different aspects of the person of Mary, namely her virginity and her role as mother. This presents a dilemma for today's women who are:

> Invited to imitate her, to aim at being pure rather than carnal, saints rather than sirens, sisters of Mary rather than daughters of Eve. Yet Mary is inimitable. Even with the greatest level of commitment and desire it is still impossible for any other woman to be both a mother and a virgin.[23]

In attempting to emulate Mary women are naturally going to fail. In addition to this, it has been suggested that some have come to believe that the veneration for Mary is a way of subtly inculcating women to accept an inferior role.[24] Mary is meek and self-effacing, humble and obedient, so to set her up as the paragon of how women should be is to emphasize a stereotypical and restrictive role for women.

A Figure for Feminist Theology and an Obedient Disciple

It is perhaps surprising to learn that whilst some have viewed Mary as a negative figure for feminism, others have welcomed her on board for feminist theology. If we understand feminist theology to be a reinterpretation of 'male' theology, which seeks to redress the balance of women's experience being relegated or excluded, then it is easy to understand that Mary, simply by virtue of being a woman, plays a role in feminist theology. Biblical feminist Elaine Storkey argues that whilst in one sense Mary's virginity is a symbol of her autonomy, we need to rediscover Mary simply as a woman. It is not as an untouchable mystery, or a symbol of purity and chastity or an example of exemplary motherhood that we should engage with Mary, but simply as a woman.[25]

Storkey also counters some of the objections, often by feminists, to the implicit submissive figure of Mary and dismisses these objections:

> There is nothing demeaning in the notion of Mary bearing her own Saviour. It is not an assertion of the supremacy of maleness or the arrogance of patriarchy. It is simply a statement of the humility of a non-gendered God who was prepared to come in human, sexual form. The virgin birth has also nothing to do with the evil of female sexuality, but everything to do with the crucial understanding of the Christ-child: both fully human and divine.[26]

It is refreshing to consider Mary in this liberating way, to embrace the social change and the sexual revolution that has taken place in secular society and to give prominence to a woman. There is clearly a point at which this reverence needs to stop—Mary bore Christ, she was not the Saviour herself, yet as a woman and a virgin she endorses a place of dignity for women independent from the roles of wife or mother.

Mary has much to teach us about being an obedient disciple

On another positive note, Mary has much to teach us about being an obedient disciple. This role she plays independently of her gender; in loving and trusting God she is eager to submit to his will: 'Let it be with me according to your word' (Luke 1:38). Modern theologian Peter Toon, in his article 'Appreciating Mary Today' considers Mark 3.31–5 and regards Jesus' words 'Whoever does the will of God is my brother and sister and mother' as a positive affirmation of Mary's obedient discipleship. Blessedness, Toon argues, is not being Jesus' mother but being an obedient disciple.[27] Mary is indeed the example for all Christians to follow in her dealings with God for she recognized and accepted her role as the handmaid of the Lord. Her obedience and submission are qualities to be aimed at by Christians of any era and at any level of spiritual maturity.[28]

It has become apparent that it is highly possible to consider Mary as a positive figure in Protestant theology not just as a virgin and a mother, but also as an obedient disciple to emulate, and as a woman with dignity and autonomy. With this interpretation in mind, it does seem appropriate to consider Mary on Mothering Sunday. It is particularly important to consider Mary's painful experience as a mother, as one who would have her own soul pierced, and would weep at the foot of her son's cross. Many churches have some kind of depiction of Mary and this could be the focus for those who need to mourn or grieve in some way on Mothering Sunday. People could be encouraged to lay flowers near Mary's depiction, as they are given the opportunity to engage with their own heartache and sorrow as they also remember Mary's. It would also be fitting for cards with the words of the Magnificat to be given to those laying flowers as a reminder of God's might and mercy even in the midst of our own sorrow.

God as Our Mother

6

One further traditional element of Mothering Sunday that needs looking at is the concept of the motherhood of God.

Interestingly, when we consider Mothering Sunday we think of flowers or of home-made cards and the notion that motherhood is a fitting subject for theological reflection or one which can teach us about the nature and saving activity of God may be less likely to cross our minds.[29]

Yet the image of God as a mother is rooted in Scripture. As Phillip Tovey outlines, the images range from God as mother of wisdom, as the mother bird who helps us fly, as the one who gives birth to us, carries and nurtures us.[30] Unfortunately, however, these images had, until the recent introduction of *Common Worship*, been largely left out of liturgy. Indeed, in the ASB there does not seem to be one instance of the use of feminine imagery in prayer to God in the whole book.[31] This has meant that reference to God and images of God have been largely patriarchal—God as King, Lord, Father. Happily, this omission has, to an extent, been redressed through *Common Worship*. Eucharistic prayer G includes reference to Matthew 23.37, Jesus' identification with a mother hen gathering her chicks. Canticle 77, 'A Song of St Anselm' also uses this metaphor, and includes the line:

> Jesus, like a mother you gather your people to you;
> you are gentle with us as a mother with her children.
>
> (For a fuller extract of this canticle see chapter 8)

Similarly, Canticle 78 'A Song of Julian of Norwich' focuses predominantly on an analogy of Christ as our mother. This inclusion of two of the best known medieval writers on the motherhood of God is a welcome means by which to explore, within liturgy, the implications and resonance of God as our mother.

Julian of Norwich argues that the use of mother terminology in relation to Jesus as 'mother' is an utterly natural and appropriate use of the word and she goes on to consider the motherhood of God in three ways. First, Jesus is our mother because he created us; 'we owe our being to him—and this is the essence of motherhood.'[32] Julian draws a parallel between labour pains and Christ's death on the cross and her image evokes the idea of a patient God who is faithful to creation even to the extent of bringing about a new birth.

Second, Julian argues that Jesus is our mother because he is the one who nurtures us. We are fed with the food from Jesus' own body, the sacrament of his body and blood, and we are clothed with his love. It is through this nurturing that we realise we are dependent on God for our survival, and receive the love of a mother God who provides for us and sustains us.

Last, Julian considers that Jesus is our mother because he liberates us. It is through God's understanding of our characters and our needs that he is able to allow us to develop and grow. Julian likens this to the way in which a mother allows a child to make mistakes in order to learn, yet not to a dangerous extent. 'But because she loves the child she will never allow the situation to become dangerous...Our heavenly Mother, Jesus, will never let us, his children, die.' This is the liberating love of God.

It is through God's understanding of our characters and our needs that he is able to allow us to develop and grow

How then is this concept of the motherhood of God, or indeed Christ, relevant to Mothering Sunday? The answer is in part due to God's understanding of all our situations and experiences, however varied they may be. The church seems to have a tendency to polarize the experience of women in relation to motherhood. To suggest that there are, on the one hand, women who have children and find the experience joyful, life affirming, and ultimately fulfilling—and on the other hand women for whom the lack of, or death of children is a tragic, life-damaging experience. Margaret Hebblethwaite paints an evocative picture that warns against such polarization and conjures an understanding of the strains and failures of motherhood:

> The feelings of a mother whose child is dead go beyond all depths of grief, but every mother shares a little in this who feels she has lost a part of her child's life. Those days that should have been so happy to-gether—irrevocably gone, spoiled by resentment and frustration—for these she will grieve and wish it had been otherwise.[33]

It is, Hebblethwaite argues, an understanding of God as our mother that enables redemption and reconciliation through these times of failure and grief. A bridge between the hopes and promises of the past and the disillusionment of the present can be found in the mother-love of God.

> God will understand all, forgive all, share with us in all, and her tenderness will never crack…In her there will always be new springs of maternal love, that we can always draw from.[34]

This brings another helpful element to Mothering Sunday—a permission to fail, and a promise of grace, acceptance and forgiveness. This may well be specifically in relation to biological mothers, but may also extend to all those—fathers, grandparents, adoptive parents and so on—involved in the raising of children. (Suggestion is made in chapter 8 as to how this may be incorporated into the liturgy of a Mothering Sunday service.) Julian's language of God as mother not only broadens and enhances our understanding of God, but also affirms that the role of mother is a godly one, one to be undertaken in imitation of Christ, and is not simply a biological role.

This brings another helpful element to Mothering Sunday— a permission to fail, and a promise of grace

7   The Negative Psychological Impact of Mothering Sunday

There are no doubt many difficult days in the church's calendar when people experience their painful memories being brought to the forefront of their minds.

Mothering Sunday seems, however, to affect a great number and variety of people. Mary Stimming evocatively captures some of the many people affected as she reflects on the customs of Mothering Sunday:

> Imagine how these rituals are received by the couple that has buried a child or experienced a miscarriage or stillbirth; the single person who longs for a spouse and children; the woman who has undergone an abortion or placed a child for adoption; the child who has buried a mother or is witnessing a mother's illness; the mother who is alienated from her children or the child estranged from his or her mother; the stepmother who has not yet found her place in the family or the mother not awarded parental custody.[35]

As this extract so ably highlights, there is a great diversity of people for whom Mothering Sunday is painful. Some of the situations as highlighted above are modern day phenomena, such as abortion and step-families, but one group for whom the day would be painful, those who can't have children, is well documented in the Bible. From Sarah in the Old Testament to Elizabeth in the New Testament there are a number of barren women in the Bible.

Scripturally, barrenness was seen as a curse and humiliation whilst fruitfulness was viewed as a reward for obedience. In the vast majority of biblical cases (and indeed in the two cases mentioned above) a son was provided as reward for the woman's faithfulness. Indeed, there are only two women other than priestesses who, we are told, remain childless:

> Tamar was raped by her brother Amnon and lived the rest of her life 'a desolate woman.' Jepthah's daughter, a virgin, was killed by her father as a result of his foolish vow. These are the childless women of Scripture.[36]

Not only are modern infertile women faced with a day devoted entirely to honouring what they can never be, but as these women turn to the pages of the Bible for comfort, they find little solace in the experience of the barren women they encounter.

As modern infertile women turn to the Bible for comfort, they find little solace in the experience of the barren women they encounter

It is, therefore, perhaps not surprising that many women decide not to attend church on Mothering Sunday:

> On Mother's day I mourn my mother's untimely death. On Mother's Day I grieve my inability to bear children. On Mother's Day I need the comfort, strength and challenge of my faith—as well as the company of believers. On Mother's Day I will not attend Mass.[37]

Surely it is the church's role to avoid the banality and superficiality that so often accompany significant moments in people's lives

It is ironic that the day when the strength of one's faith and the fellowship of other Christians is needed is also the day that church is, for many, a no-go area. This is simply not acceptable. As Stimming writes, 'As one whose heart is filled with sorrow on this day, I understand. As a theologian, I am deeply troubled.' Stimming suggests that on Mothering Sunday (and on Christmas Day) Christianity seems to sink into superficiality and sentimentalism, and that 'we fail to recognize the complex realities of life that make these two days especially difficult and distressing.'[38] Surely it is the church's role to avoid the banality and superficiality that so often accompany significant moments in people's lives. On Mothering Sunday, as well as honouring and rejoicing in mothers, the liturgy can acknowledge and comfort those who do not share this joy.

In part as a reaction to the lack of such liturgy, in 2003 Greyfriars Church in Reading introduced a service called 'Unfulfilled Dreams' on the Sunday afternoon before Mothering Sunday for all those who were grieving the loss of children or unable to have children. As part of the service the following prayer was said:

> Father of the fatherless and God of compassion
> I bring to You the grief for that which I have never had
> …and the ache and sorrow of all my losses.

I sit with empty arms wondering about the child that never was.
I sit with empty arms pondering my unfulfilled dreams.
I sit with empty arms aching with the pain of my goodbyes.
Father of the fatherless and God of compassion
I sit with empty arms trusting that your love will
    embrace my pain, shelter my vulnerability,
    and give meaning to my countless days ahead.[39]

Perhaps however the fitting place for this kind of prayer is on Mothering Sunday itself, as a way of the church embracing the emotions of all

This liturgy brilliantly captures the sorrow of many on Mothering Sunday, and allows space for grieving. Perhaps however, the fitting place for this kind of prayer is on Mothering Sunday itself, as an acknowledgement of the pain of the day, and as a way of the church embracing the emotions of *all*, rejoicing with those who rejoice and mourning with those who mourn.

Doing Mothering Sunday

Having considered three important and traditional aspects of Mothering Sunday it is interesting to approach the recent liturgical guideline for Mothering Sunday in *New Patterns for Worship* in relation to those aspects—Mother Church, Mary, Mother of God and God as our Mother.

God As Our Mother

There is a significant emphasis in the service on God as our mother. The service opens with the acclamation: 'Praise God who loves us. **Praise God who cares for us.**'[40] This immediately, albeit subtly, puts the emphasis on God's maternal and caring role. This is a focus that continues throughout much of the service, and effectively conveys the understanding of God as our mother. The Song of St Anselm which occurs in the service after the readings does this in a particularly evocative way:

> **Gather your little ones to you, O God,**
> **As a hen gathers her brood to protect them.**
> Jesus, like a mother you gather your people to you;
> you are gentle with us as a mother with her children.
> Often you weep over our sins and our pride,
> tenderly you draw us from hatred and judgement.
> You comfort us in sorrow and bind up our wounds,
> in sickness you nurse us and with pure milk you feed us.[41]

These words help to emphasise the nurturing and liberating role of our loving Mother God. In the preface to the Peace, through the words of Isaiah—'As a mother comforts her child, so I will comfort you'[42]—we are also able to consider the comforting nature of God, especially relevant on a painful day.

As a recognition of the forgiving and understanding place of God as our mother it would also be appropriate to include in the confession an acknowledgement of our failures as mothers and carers:

> You offer us understanding and grace. We fail to be gracious to those who rely on us.
> Lord, have mercy
> **All   Lord, have mercy**

These words, or equivalent, help to express the need of help we have in living
up to the example of the mother-love of God.

Mary, Mother of God

Mary is referred to, albeit briefly, at different intervals throughout the service.
Generally the references to Mary serve as a reminder that Christ had a human
mother and family and thus understands the stresses and strains of family life.
Mary herself could figure more prominently, particularly as a preface to any
parts of the service that choose to mention the pain and sacrifice of mothering
or that deal with the issue of loss.

Mother Church

Disappointingly, this service makes no reference to Mother Church or to the
issues of church unity and mothering that go with the concept. Naturally a
sermon could focus on the topic, but it would do so more effectively if this
were pointed to in the structure and content of the whole service. It would
be fitting to start the church service with an expression of church unity, or
to precede the creed with some words affirming our common faith in Christ
and belonging to Mother Church. Opportunity could also be taken during the
prayers to intercede for the church locally, nationally and worldwide. Whilst
this is probably done on an ordinary service, it would be especially poignant
on a day that honours Mother Church.

Non-verbal Liturgy

It is common practice in most Mothering Sunday services to distribute flowers
to mothers, or indeed all women, yet the distribution of flowers is probably
the most difficult part of the Mothering Sunday service. In the *New Patterns*
outline the prayers preceding the distribution are rather insensitive. The five
short prayers all focus on the experience of mothers, thanking God for their
patience, their love, their service:

For the care of mothers; **Thanks be to God.**
For their patience when tested; **Thanks be to God.**
For their love when tired; **Thanks be to God.**
For their hope when despairing; **Thanks be to God.**
For their service without limit; **Thanks be to God.**[43]

The liturgy needs, however, to cover the heartbreak of mothering as well, thus additional prayers could follow a theme similar to the ones outline below:

For those unable to have children; **Comfort them O God.**
For those who have lost children; **Comfort them O God.**
For those experiencing broken relationships; **Comfort them O God.**
For those who mourn the loss of their mothers; **Comfort them O God.**
For those who find this day difficult; **Comfort them O God.**

The difficulty of the giving of flowers is acknowledged in the guidelines for this service: 'it is important that this element of the service is conducted with sensitivity.'[44] Yet no suggestions are made as to how to be sensitive. Customarily, mothers are asked to stand, are prayed for and then given flowers. This more recently has extended into all women (married, single, mothers or childless) being given posies once the mothers have been prayed for. This is a tradition which proves highly uncomfortable for the many women who by choice or otherwise have no children and yet who are presented with flowers so as not to be left out!

Alternatively, rather than giving flowers, people could be encouraged to give a gift to someone who has played a mothering role, either in an individual's life or in the life of the church. Naturally this practice would need to be preceded by some teaching on mothering, but it would work as a way of honouring those who nurture and care for others. It seems highly fitting that on Mothering Sunday, the churchwarden who has, for years, cared for and 'mothered' the church in and through all sorts of situations should be thanked. Or the elderly spinster who has dedicated a portion of her Sundays for the last 20 years to making the congregation tea and coffee should also be recognized for her mothering role. The bestowing of flowers on mothers has been an integral part of Mothering Sunday for centuries, yet to broaden the reasoning behind this act would be both an opportunity to thank those whose service can otherwise be overlooked and would diminish the pain experienced by those for whom a biological emphasis on motherhood is difficult.

Perhaps opportunity could also be made for those who would like to offer Christ their painful experiences of motherhood could be encouraged to do so. At St Matthew's Church, Grandpont, Oxford, people wishing to do just this are offered the opportunity to light a candle and place it in a tray marked out in the shape of the cross. This has proved to be a moving and highly appropriate addition to the Mothering Sunday service. This, or a similar custom, would be appropriate to do during a hymn, or indeed during communion as people return from receiving the bread and wine.

In addition, the notion of mothering could be picked up in the banners or other visual aids in the church. If we concentrate on Cunnee's definition of mothering as a sympathy for others that leads to thought and action, images around the church denoting various acts of service could affirm everyone's role in 'mothering' others. Furthermore, as a way of remembering and honouring women and men who have lost mothers and indeed children, there could be a special flower arrangement. This could be put together with the involvement of the bereaved with flowers chosen by remaining families to represent their lost ones.

Mission

All of this has so far concentrated on the congregation that normally gathers at church, yet Mothering Sunday is also a day in which to focus on non-church-goers. It is an opportunity to invite back baptism families to the service, to celebrate their family units (perhaps with cake!) and to pray for the care and nurture that goes on in their homes. It is an opportunity to invite members of the community who have a mothering role in order to acknowledge and thank them for the work they do. It is also an opportunity to meet and support those who visit the churchyard in order to lay flowers on mothers' or children's graves. This support could take the form of providing the flowers, offering bereavement counselling or simply a cup of tea. Importantly, however, the focus of Mothering Sunday need not simply be on those used to attending church.

Summary

Overall the service for Mothering Sunday from *New Patterns* is a thoughtful one. It avoids stereotyping the role of mothers as some material in *Together for Festivals: A Resource Anthology* does. One particularly worrying example of this is a choral piece by Peter Charlton entitled 'Thanks Mum' which focuses solely on appreciating mothers for the endless chores they do in the home:

> Thanks very much for doing so much shopping
> Thanks very much for cooking so much food,
> Thanks very much for washing up the dishes
> When Dad and me just weren't in the mood. [45]

This emphasis would be highly insulting for a number of mothers and misses much of the historical and theological basis for Mothering Sunday. In contrast, the *New Patterns* service places an important emphasis on God as our mother, though it is disappointing that the service does not mention Mother Church or church unity and skims over the role of Mary. The service is also rather unbalanced, affirming mothers but not the pain of mothering or the 'mothering' that most do for others. It is also interesting that *New Patterns of Worship* has a service outline for Father's Day, in which there is no specific accolade for fathers, no distribution of gifts and no prayers for fathers. Father's day is not a part of the church's calendar, but if we choose to recognise it and honour fathers, why do we not do so in the same way we celebrate Mothering Sunday?

Conclusion

9

'My family and I try to avoid church on Mothering Sunday. My wife died a few years ago, so now I am both mother and father to my children. But there is no place for me or for my children's grief in the celebrations of the Mothering Sunday Service.'

These are sentiments expressed by someone whose own personal experience clashes resoundingly with the content of a traditional service on Mothering Sunday. Unfortunately, the modern focus has moved away from the day's origins and now concentrates almost solely on our earthly mothers. One effect of this has been that Mothering Sunday has become a painful day for a wide variety of church members: for those without mothers or without children; for those with difficult experiences of motherhood or childhood; for those involved in demanding mothering roles without being biological mothers themselves—to name but a few. For many of these people there is a temptation to avoid church completely on Mothering Sunday.

To remove the focus from mothers entirely would be unfair and disrespectful. The experience of mothers in today's culture is, as we have seen, difficult and demanding, and motherhood itself can be fraught with tension, perceived failures and heartache. The church, therefore, needs to embrace this tension and broaden once again the focus of the day. In focusing on Mother Church it is possible to affirm the unity of the church, unified in praise of God who nurtures and cares for us. This leads also to a recognition of the mothering role played by all church members regardless of gender or status, seeking to empower one another and enabling growth in individuals and the church as a whole.

A focus on Mary is a reminder of an obedient disciple, ready and willing to do God's will, yet touched also by the heartache and confusion of loss. Last, a reminder of God as our mother reiterates the love, understanding, grace and forgiveness offered to all God's children. This is a God whose maternal example inspires the relationships we have with others, whilst offering reconciliation and redemption for the mistakes we have made. All of these elements are important inclusions for a broad understanding of Mothering Sunday and can be permeated through the service in verbal and non-verbal liturgy. It is this balance of emphasis that ensures Mothering Sunday can remain an appropriate celebration for the church, a celebration to which all individuals will be drawn regardless of their own personal experience. It is this balance that will ensure the church stops inflicting additional pain on those who had wished to avoid the service altogether, but rather will offer comfort, solace or indeed celebration on this special day.

Bibliography

Books and Articles:

Abbot, Walter M (ed), *The Documents of Vatican II* (Western Printing, 1966)

Caudwell, Irene, *Ceremonies of Holy Church* (London: The Faith Press, 1948)

Braaten, Carl E, *Mother Church: Ecology and Ecumenism* (Minneapolis: Fortress Press, 1998)

Cunnee, Sally, *Mother Church: What the Experience of Women is Teaching Her* (Paulist Press, 1991)

Currie, H, '"Mothering" Sunday: a Philological Conjecture' in *Expository Times* 104, 1993

Currie, Nicola and Thompson, Jean, *Seasons, Saints and Sticky Tape* (Church House Publishing, 1992)

Dunn, J D G, *The Epistle to the Galatians* (London: A & C Black Publishers Ltd, 1993)

Hebblethwaite, Margaret, *Motherhood and God* (Cassell Publishers, 1984)

Julian of Norwich, *Revelations of Divine Love* (Penguin Books Ltd, 1966)

McAllaster, Elva, 'His Mother: Learning from Mary, the maternal model.' From *Christianity Today* May 12, 1972 found on http://www.christianitytoday.com/ct/2000/119/56.0.html

Mackall, Dandi Daley, 'The Mother in Me.' From *Today's Christian Woman Magazine* May/June 1997, Vol 19 No 3 found on http://www.christianitytoday.com/tcw/7w3/7w3048.html

Macquarrie, John, *Mary for All Christians* (T&T Clark, 1990 2nd Edition 2001)

Moessner, Jeanne Stevenson, 'The Pink Rose' in *Journal for Preachers* 21.03 (© 2001 ATLA Serials)

New Patterns for Worship, (Church House Publishing, 2002)

Sayers, Susan, *Living Stones: Complete Resource Book Year A* (Kevin Mayhew Ltd, 1998)

Schmidt, Leigh E, 'Piety, Commercialism, Activism: The Uses of Mothers Day' in *The Christian Century* 108.16

Slee, Nicola, 'The Motherhood of God' in *Expository Times* 102, 1991

Smith, Constance Penswick, 'A Short History of Mothering Sunday' 2nd Edition (Nottingham, 1925) in *12 Pamphlets on Festivals 1850–1933*

Smith, Constance Penswick, 'More about Mothering Sunday' (Nottingham, 1928) in *12 Pamphlets on Festivals 1850–1933*

Smith, Constance Penswick, *The Revival of Mothering Sunday* (Nottingham, 1921 2nd edition 1932)

Stimming, Mary T, 'Crucifixion Amnesia: Left out on Mother's Day' in *Christian Century* 114.15 (© 2001, ATLA Serials) May 7, 1997

Together for Festivals 2: A Resource Anthology (Church House Publishing, 1987)

Tovey, Phillip, *Praying to God as Mother* (Grove Spirituality booklet S 38, 1991)

Wright, David (ed), *Chosen By God: Mary in Evangelical Perspective* (Marshall Pickering, 1989)

Websites:

http://www.jrf.org.uk/knowledge/findings/socialpolicy/sp106.asp

http://www.21stcenturyplaza.com/taste/mothers.html

Notes

1   For the full survey results see http://www.jrf.org.uk/knowledge/findings/socialpolicy/sp106.asp
2   Constance Penswick Smith, *The Revival of Mothering Sunday* (Nottingham, 1921 2nd edition 1932) p 45–46
3   Nicola Currie and Jean Thompson, *Seasons, Saints and Sticky Tape* (Church House Publishing, 1992) p 31
4   Smith, *The Revival* p 12
5   It is worth noting in passing that Smith's numerous booklets on Mothering Sunday were borne out of the Mothering Sunday Movement (see 1. vi) and are concerned to refer people back to the origins of the day. She is not intending to write a detailed history, thus many of her assertions are not substantiated.
6   Cutts, as quoted in Smith, *A Short History* p 6
7   Smith, *A Short History* p 7
8   JDG Dunn, *The Epistle to the Galatians* (1993, A & C Black Publishers ltd, London) p 254
9   Carl E Braaten, *Mother Church: Ecology and Ecumenism* (Fortress Press, Minneapolis, 1998) p 1
10 As quoted in Braaten, *Mother Church*, p 2
11 As quoted in Braaten, *Mother Church*, p 2
12 As quoted in Braaten, *Mother Church*, p 3
13 Sally Cunnee, *Mother Church: What the Experience of Women is Teaching Her* (Paulist Press, 1991) p 3
14 Braaten, *Mother Church*, p 2
15 Smith, *The Revival*, p 19
16 Cunnee *Mother Church* p 31
17 Cunnee, *Mother Church* p 8
18 David Wright, 'Introduction: The Problem of Mary' in David Wright (ed), *Chosen By God: Mary in Evangelical Perspective* (Marshall Pickering, 1989) p 1
19 Elva McAllaster, 'His Mother: Learning from Mary, the maternal model.' From *Christianity Today* May 12, 1972 found on http://www.christianitytoday.com/ct/2000/119/56.0.html
20 Walter M Abbot (ed), *The Documents of Vatican II* (Western Printing, 1966) p 88
21 David Wright, 'Mother of God' in Wright, *Chosen by God*, p 137
22 *Documents of Vatican II* p 96, 630
23 Elaine Storkey, 'The Significance of Mary for Feminist Theology' in Wright *Chosen by God* p 189
24 John Macquarrie, *Mary for All Christians* (T&T Clark, 1990 2nd Edition 2001) p 8
25 Storkey 'The Significance of Mary' p 196
26 Storkey, 'The Significance of Mary' p 198
27 Toon, 'Appreciating Mary Today' in Wright, *Chosen By God*, p 218–9
28 Elva McAllaster, 'His Mother: Learning from Mary, the maternal model.'
29 Nicola Slee, 'The Motherhood of God' in *Expository Times* 102, 1991 p 142
30 Phillip Tovey, *Praying to God as Mother* (Grove Books, 1991) p 13
31 Tovey, *Praying to God as Mother*, p 7
32 Julian of Norwich, *Revelations of Divine Love* (Penguin Books Ltd, 1966) p 16
33 Margaret Hebblethwaite, *Motherhood and God* (Cassell Publishers, 1984) p 64
34 Hebblethwaite, *Motherhood and God*, p 69
35 Mary T Stimming, 'Crucifixion Amnesia: Left out on Mother's Day' in *Christian Century* 114.15 (© 2001, ATLA Serials) May 7, 1997 p 436
36 Jeanne Stevenson Moessner, 'The Pink Rose' in *Journal for Preachers* 21.03 (© 2001 ATLA Serials)
37 Stimming, 'Crucifixion Amnesia' p 436
38 Stimming, 'Crucifixion Amnesia' 436
39 Provided by the church
40 *New Patterns for Worship*, (Church House Publishing, 2002) p 418 The words in bold are those to be said by the congregation, those in normal type are said by the minister.
41 *New Patterns for Worship*, p 419
42 *New Patterns for Worship* p 422
43 *New Patterns for Worship* p 422
44 *New Patterns for Worship* p 417
45 *Together for Festivals 2: A Resource Anthology* (Church House Publishing, 1987)